The Hot Salsa Cookbook

50 Easy, Flavorful Recipes for Appetizers, Salads, Main Dishes and more

Angelina Baker

The following Book is reproduced below with the goal of providing information that is as accurate and reliable as possible. Regardless, purchasing this Book can be seen as consent to the fact that both the publisher and the author of this book are in no way experts on topics discussed within and that any recommendations or suggestions that are made herein are for entertainment purposes only.

Professionals should be consulted as needed prior to undertaking any of the action endorsed herein.

This declaration is deemed fair and valid by both the American Bar Association and the Committee of Publishers Association and is legally binding throughout the United States.

Furthermore, the transmission, duplication, or reproduction of any of the following work including specific information will be considered an illegal act irrespective of if it is done electronically or in print. This extends to creating a secondary or tertiary copy of the work or a recorded copy and is only allowed with the express written consent from the Publisher. All additional right reserved.

The information in the following pages is broadly considered a truthful and accurate account of facts and as such, any inattention, use, or misuse of the information in question by the reader will render any resulting actions solely under their purview.

There are no scenarios in which the publisher or the original author of this work can be in any fashion deemed liable for any hardship or damages that may befall them after undertaking information described herein.

Additionally, the information in the following pages is intended only for informational purposes and should thus be thought of as universal. As befitting its nature, it is presented without assurance regarding its prolonged validity or interim quality. Trademarks that are mentioned are done without written consent and can in no way be considered an endorsement from the trademark holder.

Table of Contents

Tomato and Mango Salsa Recipe

Ingredients

- 1 small mango
- 1 large tomato, seeded and chopped
- 1/3 cup chopped red onion
- 1/4 cup minced fresh cilantro
- 1 small jalapeno pepper, seeded and finely chopped
- 2 tablespoons lime juice

Method

Carefully peel skin from mango sections attached to seed.

Slice flesh from seed. Chop flesh to measure 1-1/2 cups.

Combine all ingredients in small bowl; refrigerate 2 hours.

Carrot Mango Salsa Recipe

- 4oz carrots
- 1 ripe mango (diced, skinned, pit discarded)
- 1 small onion sliced
- 14oz diced apricots
- 2 tablespoons lime juice
- 1 tablespoon sugar
- 1 teaspoon ground cumin
- half a red pepper
- 1 green chili (seeded, chopped)

Method

Add all ingredients together, stir well for a minute.

Serve warmed or chilled as a condiment with chicken or fish.

RED HOT SALSA Recipe

Ingredients

- 1 (16 oz.) can tomatoes or 6 peeled
- fresh tomatoes (if in season)
- 1/2 sm. onion, diced
- 2 jalapeno peppers, chopped
- 2 garlic cloves, minced
- 1 tsp. sugar
- 1 tsp. chili powder
- 1/2 tsp. salt (more or less)
- 1/2 tsp. black pepper
- 1 tbsp. cilantro
- 2 tbsp. apple cider vinegar

Method

Combine all ingredients in food processor or blender and mix for 10-15 seconds or until all ingredients are of desired consistency.

Serve with tortilla chips or as sauce on assorted foods.

Salsa Italiano

Ingredients

- 1 lb. (2 large) fresh tomatoes, seeded and diced
- 1/2 cup chopped red onion
- 1 can (2.25 oz.) sliced ripe olives
- 1 jar (6 oz.) marinated artichoke hearts
- 2 Tbsp. lemon juice
- 2 garlic cloves, finely chopped
- 3 Tbsp. chopped fresh basil
- 1/4 tsp. crushed hot red pepper flakes
- 1/4 tsp. salt
- 1/8 tsp. ground black pepper

Method

In a medium bowl, combine tomato, onion and olives.

Slice artichoke hearts, reserving marinade.

Stir sliced artichoke hearts into tomato mixture; set aside.

In a small bowl, whisk together lemon juice, garlic, basil, pepper flakes, salt, black pepper, and 2 Tbsp artichoke marinade.

Gently mix dressing with tomato mixture. Serve with roast or barbecued chicken.

Black and White Salsa

Ingredients

- 1-1/2 Cups Cooked and Drained Black Beans or 1 16-ounce Can Black
- Beans, Drained
- 1-1/2 Cups Cooked and Drained Great Northern Beans or 1 16-ounce Can
- Great Northern Beans
- 1 Cup Diced Tomatoes
- 3 Tablespoons White Wine Vinegar
- 1/4 Cup Chipped Cilantro
- 1/4 Cup Chopped Red Onion
- 2 Tablespoons Chopped Jalapeno Pepper
- 2 Cloves Garlic, Minced
- 1/2 Teaspoon Salt and Sugar
- 1/8 Teaspoon Ground Black Pepper

Method

In medium bowl, toss everything together.

Serve with roast or barbecued chicken.

Pineapple Salsa

Ingredients

- 2 cans pineapple chunks drained
- 1 jalapeno cored seeded
- 1 red bell pepper cored seeded
- 1 lime-rolled, cut and squeezed
- 1 sprig fresh cilantro
- pinch of salt
- few twists of black pepper
- 1 tablespoon of ex virgin olive oil

Method

Toss all ingredients into a processor and mix well.

Serve over grilled fish or with chips.

Creamy Salsa Dip

Ingredients

- 2 cups Plain Yogurt
- 1 cup prepared salsa
- 3 tablespoons chopped fresh cilantro
- 1 teaspoon salt

Method

In a small bowl, combine yogurt and salsa. Mix well.

Stir in cilantro and salt.

Cover and keep refrigerated until ready to use!

Salsa Cheeseburgers

Ingredients

- 1 package (about 1 1/4 pounds) PERDUE? FIT 'N EASY?
- Fresh Ground Turkey Breast Meat, Ground Turkey, or Ground Chicken
- 1 cup Spicy Salsa (recipe follows) or prepared tomato salsa, well drained
- 1 tablespoon chopped cilantro
- 1/4 teaspoon salt
- 3/4 cup shredded Cheddar cheese
- 8 slices French or Italian bread or 4 hamburger rolls
- Mayonnaise
- Shredded lettuce
- Avocado slices
- Red onion slices
- Additional Spicy Salsa (optional)
- Lime or lemon wedges (optional)

Method

Prepare outdoor grill for cooking or preheat broiler.

In medium bowl, combine ground turkey, 1 cup salsa, cilantro and salt. Form turkey mixture into 4 burgers.

Grill or broil burgers 5 to 6 inches from heat source 5 minutes on each side or until no longer pink in center.

Just before removing burgers from grill, sprinkle cheese over tops; cover and cook about 1 minute or until cheese melts.

Grill or broil bread lightly, if desired. Serve burgers between bread slices, topping burgers with choice of mayonnaise, shredded lettuce, avocado slices, red onion slices and/or additional salsa.

Garnish with lime or lemon wedges.

Spicy Salsa (optional):

In medium bowl, combine 1-pound ripe plum tomatoes (about 5), seeded, and finely chopped, 1/4 cup minced white or yellow onion, 1 fresh hot green chili pepper, seeded and minced or 2 tablespoons canned chopped green chilies, 1 garlic clove, minced, 2 tablespoons lime juice, 1 tablespoon chopped fresh cilantro (coriander) sprigs (optional) and salt to taste.

Cover and refrigerate 30 minutes or up to 24 hours before serving; longer storage can reduce salsa's fresh flavor and texture. Makes about 1 cup.

Ready In: 45 minutes

Servings: Makes 4 servings

Salsa Chicken Sandwiches

Ingredients

- 1 package (10 1/2 ounces) frozen breaded chicken breast patties
- 4 whole wheat sandwich buns, split
- 8 teaspoons purchased black bean dip
- 1/4 cup thick-and-chunky salsa
- 1/2 cup shredded lettuce

Method

Cook chicken in oven as directed on package, adding buns, cut side up, last 3 to 4 minutes of cooking time until lightly toasted.

Spread bottom half of each bun with 2 teaspoons dip. Top each with Chicken patty; spread with 1 tablespoon salsa.

Top each with 2 tablespoons Lettuce and top of bun.

Makes 4 sandwiches.

Mexican Food to Go Favourite Salsa Recipes

Ingredients

- 4 medium tomatoes, peeled and chopped
- 1/2 cup finely chopped onion (up to 1 cup)
- 1/2 cup finely chopped celery
- 1/4 cup finely chopped green pepper (bell pepper)
- 1/4 cup oil
- 2 tbsp finely chopped green chiles
- 2 tbsp red wine vinegar
- 1 tsp mustard seed
- 1 tsp cilantro (coriander) seed, crushed (or fresh cilantro leaves)
- 1 tsp salt

Method

Combine all ingredients. Cover and chill, stirring occasionally. Serve with corn chips.

Mango Salsa Recipe

Ingredients

- 1 large Mango; peeled -- 1/4" cubed
- 1/4 cup red bell pepper -- 1/4" diced
- 1 1/2 tbsp fresh basil -- finely chopped
- 1 1/2 tbsp red wine vinegar
- 2 tsp lime juice
- 1/2 tsp sugar
- 1 Jalapeno pepper (opt) -- finely chopped.
- seeds and membranes -- discarded

Method

In a medium bowl, combine all ingredients. Mix well.

Let stand at room temperature a half hour before serving or refrigerate up to 24 hours.

Two Tomato Salsa

Ingredients

- 2 c diced unpeeled plum tomato
- 1 c unpeeled green tomato
- 1/2 c diced green bell pepper
- 1/4 c chopped purple onion
- 1 tbsp finely chop jalapeno pepper
- 1 tbsp finely chop fresh cilantro
- 1 clove minced garlic
- 1/4 tsp salt.
- 1/8 tsp coarsely ground pepper
- 2 tbsp fresh lime juice
- 1 tbsp olive oil

Method

Combine all ingredients in a bowl. Stir well. Serve at room temperature or chilled.

Use a slotted spoon to serve with corn tortilla wedges, poultry, or fish. Yield: 3 cups

Tropical Fruit and Black Bean Salsa Recipe

Ingredients

- 1/2 c pineapple, diced
- 1/2 c mango, diced
- 1/2 c papaya, diced
- 1/2 c onions, red, chopped
- 1/2 c onions, red, chopped
- 1/2 c beans, black, cooked
- 1 jalapeno, minced.

Method

Mix all ingredients. Allow flavors to develop for at least 30mts.

Fruit Salsa Recipe

Ingredients

- 1 cup strawberries
- 2 Granny Smith apples, peeled and chopped
- 2 kiwi fruit, peeled
- 2 tablespoons brown sugar
- 2 tablespoons apple jelly or all fruit jelly juice from 1 orange

Method

Chop all in food processor to desired consistency.
Cut a flour tortilla into bite size pieces. Spray lightly with Pam.

Dust with sugar/cinnamon mixture and toast in oven until lightly browned.

Serve as a scooper with Fruit Salsa.

Avocado-Tomato Salsa Recipe

Ingredients

- 2 tomatoes, diced
- 1/2 cup chopped red onions
- 1/4 avocado, cubed.
- 1 green chili pepper, seeded and chopped
- 2 tbsp snipped fresh parsley
- 1 tbsp red wine vinegar
- 2 tsp grated lime peel
- 1 tsp lime juice
- 1/4 tsp ground cumin

Method

Combine tomatoes, onions, avocado, peppers, parsley, vinegar, lime peel, juice, and cumin.

Let stand for 15 minutes before serving.

Yield: 6 servings.

Fruit Salsa Recipe

Ingredients

- 1 cup chopped peeled pineapple
- 1 cup chopped peeled mango
- 1 cup chopped yellow or red bell pepper
- 2/3 cup chopped peeled kiwi fruit
- 1/2 cup finely chopped red onion
- 1/4 cup finely chopped fresh cilantro
- 1 teaspoon fresh lime juice
- 1/2 teaspoon minced Serrano chili (with seeds)
- Ground white pepper

Method

Combine all ingredients in medium bowl. Season with white pepper and salt. Can be made 3 hours ahead.

Makes about 4 cups.

Fresh Tomato Salsa Recipe

Ingredients

- 4 to 6 medium tomatoes
- 2 to 3 white onions
- 1 can black olives.
- 3 to 4 green chiles
- 2 Tbsp. vinegar
- 2 Tbsp. oil.

Method

Chop tomatoes, onions, olives & green chiles in very small pieces.

Combine oil and vinegar, pour over tomato mixture.

Serve with corn or taco chips. For best flavor, chill for several hours before serving.

Tropical Fruit Salsa Recipe

Ingredients

- 1 ripe mango, peeled, pitted and cut into 1/4" cubes
- 1 ripe papaya, peeled, seeded and cut into 1/4" cubes
- 1 ripe Avocado, peeled, pitted and cut into 1/4" cubes
- 3 tbsp. lime juice
- 2 tbsp. fresh cilantro, chopped.
- 2 tbsp. brown sugar
- 1 tsp. jalapeno peppers, drained.
- 1 tsp. ginger, crushed

Method

Combine all ingredients in a medium bowl.

Cover and refrigerate at least 1 hour to allow flavors to blend. Serve with grilled fish or chicken.

Also good with tortilla chips.

Salsa De Picante Recipe

Ingredients

- 2 large cans tomatoes, chopped
- 3 small cans green chilies, chopped
- 2 small cans jalapeno peppers, chopped
- 2 large onions, chopped
- 6-10 garlic cloves, chopped
- 1 tbsp salt.

Method

Place all ingredients in a large pot and bring to a boil.

Boil for 5 minutes. Cool & refrigerate.

Habanero Salsa

Ingredients

- 2 tb Olive oil
- 1 md Onion -- chopped
- 1 Green bell pepper -- chopped
- 1 Red bell pepper -- chopped
- 1/2 c Chicken broth
- 4 Chiles habanero -- minced
- 6 md Tomatoes -- skinned & diced
- 2 cn Tomatoes -- diced
- 2 tb Lime juice
- 2 tb Lemon juice
- 1 ts Dried coriander leaf
- 1 ts Oregano
- 1 tb Sugar or honey -- optional
- Salt and pepper -- to taste
- 1/4 c Fresh parsley -- chopped
- 2 Anaheim chili pepper -- chopped

Method

Sauté the onions, bell peppers, and anaheims in the oil for a few minutes then add the chicken broth and sauté until the broth is about gone.

Add the habaneros (I roasted mine first), diced tomatoes (okay, I added the extra two cans to cut the heat down a bit, so if you want it super-hot you can eliminate the cans or a couple of the habaneros), lime and lemon juices, coriander, oregano, sugar, salt, and pepper.

Simmer for 20 or 30 minutes and add the parsley and simmer a few more minutes.

Hot Salsa

Ingredients

- 3 md Tomatoes
- 3 To 4 jalapeno peppers
- Onion -- your choice
- Oregano -- dash
- Salt and pepper as you like

Method

In saucepan boil tomatoes and peppers. Drain water and remove skin from tomatoes.

Put in blender with remaining ingredients and blend for a minute or until smooth, unless you prefer your salsa chunky.

Apple Berry Salsa with Cinnamon Chips

Ingredients

--- Chips ---

- 2 10-inch flour tortillas
- Water
- 1 tb Sugar
- 1 ts Cinnamon

--- Salsa ---

- 2 md Granny Smith apples -- peel/core/chop
- 1 c Strawberries -- hulled & sliced
- 1 Kiwi -- peeled and chopped
- 1 sm Orange
- 2 tb Brown sugar
- 2 tb Apple jelly

Method

Preheat oven to 475. Lightly brush one side of tortillas with water.

Combine cinnamon and sugar, sprinkle over tortillas. Cut each tortilla into 8 wedges.

Place wedges on a stone or cookie sheet.

Bake 5 - 7 minutes or until golden brown. Remove to cooling rack. While tortillas are baking, zest orange (about 2 tbsp.) and juice orange (about 1/4 cup).

Combine prepared fruit, orange zest, orange juice, brown sugar and apple jelly. Serve fruit salsa with cinnamon chips.

Original Mexican Salsa Recipe

Ingredients

- 2 Jitomates (2 tomatoes)
- 1/2 cebolla (1/2 an onion)
- 1 diente de ajo (1 clove garlic)
- chile serrano al gusto (chopped fresh chilli)
- 1tsp for mild 4 for freaking hot.

Method

Peel the tomatoes by blanching, remove the skins and scoop out the seeds.

Dice all the ingredients, season with salt and pepper serve the salsa Mexicana after at least one hour.

Spicy Jalapeno Salsa

Ingredients

- 6 jalapenos, stems/ seeds removed, chopped
- 6 tomatoes, skins and seeds removed, chopped
- 1 tsp Salt
- 1/2 White onion, chopped
- 1/2 Cup Cilantro, chopped
- 2 Cloves garlic, chopped
- 1 red pepper, roasted, skin and seeds removed and chopped fine
- 1 green pepper, roasted, skin and seeds removed and chopped fine
- 1 cucumber skinned and seeds removed then chopped fine

Method

Mix 1oz of each tequila, white wine vinegar with 2 tsp of white sugar until dissolved and toss thru the vegetable garnish. Mix well and then place in an airtight container over night before using.

Hot Salsa

Ingredients

- 1 Red onion diced fine
- 1 Red pepper diced fine
- 6 Red chilli's chopped
- 1 tsp dry chilli powder
- 2 cloves garlic crushed
- 1 tsp Salt
- 6 tomatoes skin and seed removed and diced fine
- 1 tsp Cumin seeds and 1 tsp coriander seeds crushed in a mortar and pestle.
- zest and juice from 3 limes, 2 lemons (chop zest)
- 2 tsp of brown sugar

Method

To make the hot salsa dissolve sugar in lemon juice and then mix thru all other ingredients, store covered in the fridge for 24 hours stirring occasionally.

Guadalajara Salsa

Ingredients

- 1 lb ripe tomatoes, seeded and roughly chopped
- 2 c spicy vegetable juice
- 1/2 c chili sauce
- 1 1/2 tb fresh lime juice
- 1/2 c green onions, thinly sliced
- l medium avocado, cut in inch dice
- 1 c diced jicama
- 1 c fresh corn off the cob
- 1/8 ts salt
- fresh ground pepper
- 1/2 c cilantro leaves, coarsely chopped

Method

To make the Guadalajara salsa in a blender, puree tomatoes, vegetable juice, chili sauce and lime juice until smooth. Pour into a large bowl.

Stir in onions, avocado, jicama, corn, salt and pepper. Chill the Guadalajara salsa for at least 2 hours.

Carrot Salsa

Ingredients

- 1/2 - cup baby carrots, diced
- 1 – tablespoon red onion, diced fine
- 1 – tablespoon red bell pepper, diced fine
- 1 – tablespoon yellow bell pepper, diced fine
- 1 – tablespoon cilantro, chopped
- 1 – green chile pepper, diced fine
- 1 – tablespoon fresh lemon juice
- 1/8 – teaspoon salt
- 1/2 - teaspoon fresh ground pepper

Method

In a glass-mixing bowl, you want to combine carrots, red onion, red and yellow bell pepper, cilantro, green chile, lemon juice, salt, and pepper.

Cover with plastic wrap and place in refrigerator for 30 minutes.

Pico de Gallo

Ingredients

Servings: about 4 cups

- 2 large vine-ripened tomatoes, finely diced
- 1/2 large onion, finely diced
- 1/3 cup finely chopped cilantro
- 4 large radishes, finely diced
- 2 jalapeños, seeded and finely diced
- 2 tablespoons fresh lime juice
- 1 garlic clove, minced
- 3/4 teaspoon coarse salt

Method

Combine all of the ingredients in a bowl and serve.

The Pico de Gallo can be refrigerated overnight.

Chipotle Salsa

Ingredients

Servings: about 2 Cups

- 6 small tomatillos, husked
- 5 large garlic cloves
- 4 plum tomatoes
- 1/4 large onion
- 3 canned chipotle chiles in adobo, seeded and finely chopped, with 2 teaspoons of the adobo sauce
- 3 tablespoons finely chopped fresh cilantro
- Coarse salt
- 1/2 teaspoon sugar

Method

Heat a large cast-iron skillet. When it is very hot, add the tomatillos, garlic cloves, tomatoes and onion and cook over low heat, turning frequently, until blackened in spots and softened, 8 to 10 minutes.

Transfer the vegetables to a plate and let cool.

Put the tomatillos, garlic, tomatoes and onion in a food processor and pulse until coarsely chopped.

Add the chipotles and adobo sauce, cilantro, salt and sugar and pulse just until combined.

Chipotle Pepper Sauce

Ingredients

Makes about 2 1/2 cups

- 1 medium red bell pepper
- 1/2 cup diced pineapple (1/2 inch)
- 1/2 cup diced mango (1/2 inch)
- 1/2 cup diced papaya (1/2 inch)
- 1 small starfruit, sliced 1/4 inch thick
- 1 medium jalapeño chile, seeded and minced
- 1/4 cup fresh lemon juice
- 2 tablespoons fresh lime juice
- Salt and freshly ground white pepper
- 2 tablespoons minced fresh cilantro

Method

The salsa can be refrigerated for up to 6 hours. Serve with pork, Italian sausage, chicken, any meaty or firm, white-fleshed fish, shrimp.

Roast the bell pepper over a gas flame or under a broiler, turning often, until charred.

Transfer to a paper bag and let steam for 5 minutes.

Peel the charred skin and discard the core, ribs, and seeds. Finely chop the pepper.

Combine all the ingredients except the cilantro in a medium bowl.

Stir in the cilantro and serve chilled or at room temperature.

Ultimate Nightmare Salsa

Ingredients

- 20 Roma tomatoes
- 10 cloves of roasted garlic
- 1 large onion
- 1 green pepper
- 6 chiles de Habanero
- 1/4 cup honey
- 2 teaspoons cilantro
- 2 tablespoons fresh basil
- 1tablespoon kosher salt
- 2 teaspoons white pepper

Method

Cut 10 Roma's in half across widthwise and squeeze out the seeds and stuff. Discard the juice.

Chop the tomatoes into chunks. Take the rest of the ingredients and put into a blender or food processor and rough chop.

Combine the 2 stages, mix well and refrigerate overnight. It is not necessary to let it set overnight, but it tastes so much better the following day.

I liked the honey in this recipe, it gives it a sweet and spicy flavor (I suppose spicy is quite an understatement).

House Salsa

Ingredients

- 1 bunch green onions, trimmed, cut into 1-inch pieces, and/or 1/3 cup
- red onion, chopped
- 3 cloves garlic
- 1/4 cup coarsely chopped fresh cilantro leaves
- A 4-ounce can chopped green chiles
- A 28-ounce can tomatoes, with juice (or better yet, about 2 cups chopped fresh vine-ripened tomatoes, in season)
- Juice of 1 lime
- 1 tablespoon olive oil
- 1 teaspoon seasoned salt or Cajun seasoning blend
- Additional hot stuff as desired - Tabasco, jalapeño, whatever you like...
- name your poison!

Method

Using a food processor, place the onion, garlic and cilantro leaves in the work bowl, and pulse a few times to chop.

Scrape down the sides of the bowl with a rubber spatula and add the remaining ingredients.

Pulse a few more times - enough to achieve a uniformly chunky consistency. Let the salsa ripen at room temperature for an hour or longer.

If you like a traditional "soupy" salsa, stir in 1/4 cup ice water at serving time.

Adding ice water to cool the salsa is preferable to refrigerating it, since that changes its flavor and texture for the worse.

Makes about 1 ½ to 2 cups.

Corn and Tomato Salsa

Ingredients

- 1 cup fresh corn kernels (from 2 small ears) or frozen, thawed
- 1 large tomato, seeded, chopped
- 2/3 cup chopped red onion
- 1/2 cup chopped fresh cilantro
- 2 tablespoons olive oil
- 1 tablespoon fresh lemon juice
- ½ teaspoon ground cumin
- ½ to 1 jalapeño chili, seeded, minced
- 1 avocado, pitted, peeled, chopped
- Fresh cilantro sprigs

Method

Mix all ingredients together in a large bowl, cover and chill before serving. Plum Chile Salsa.

Roasted Chicken Legs with Plum Chile Salsa

Ingredients

- 1 pound ripe purple or red plums (about 4 large), diced (about 3 cups)
- 1/3 cup minced red onion
- ½ cup finely chopped fresh cilantro
- ¼ cup finely chopped fresh mint leaves
- 1 teaspoon minced seeded fresh jalapeño (wear rubber gloves)
- 1 tablespoon fresh lime juice
- 2 teaspoons sugar, or to taste

Method

In a bowl, stir together the plums, onion, cilantro, mint, jalapeño, lime juice and sugar. Salt and pepper to taste.

Pineapple-Apricot Salsa

Ingredients

- 1 cup finely chopped peeled cored fresh pineapple
- ½ cup finely chopped red onion
- ½ cup apricot-pineapple preserves
- ¼ cup chopped fresh cilantro
- 2 tablespoons fresh lime juice
- 1-½ tablespoons minced seeded jalapeño chili

Method

Toss all ingredients in small bowl to blend.

Season with salt and pepper. Can be made one day ahead.

Cover and chill.

10 Years to Find Salsa

Ingredients

- 20 each Tomatoes - Roma
- 1 can Whole Peeled Tomatoes - Large Can
- 1 bunch Fresh Cilantro - Leaves Only
- 1 tbs Garlic Salt
- 1 tsp Cumin
- 3 each Jalapeno Peppers - the entire pepper
- 1 each Habanerro Pepper - the entire pepper
- 1 each Fresh Lime Juice - squeezed
- 1 each Large White Onion - diced small
- 1 pkg Sazon Goya Seasoning

Method for Making 10 Years to Find Salsa

It took me about 10 years to perfect this recipe. I am often told that I should market it. You must consume this within 24 hours after preparation because fresh ingredients will become bitter. ENJOY!

In blender - add tomatoes, cilantro, peppers, garlic salt, lime juice, seasoning..........everything except the onions.

Blend together at low speed. Pour into large bowl. Dice onions separately with a sharp knife, do not use blender.

Add diced onions to mixture.

Chill and serve with tortilla chips.

Note: If mixture is too thick add a little tomato juice or water. If too thin, a small can have crushed tomatoes or tomato sauce works fine.

SCARY SALSA

Ingredients

- 5 RED TOMATOES
- 5 GREEN TOMATOES
- 1 HABANARO PEPPER
- I LARGE HUNGARIAN
- WAX HOT PEPPER
- 2 CHILLIE PEPPERS
- 2 HALIPINO PEPPERS
- 2 CLOVES OF GARLIC
- 1 TLBS SALT
- 1 TLBS SUGAR. 2/3
- CUP OF WATER

Method

Prepare tomatoes as kif you were canning them. Core and skin. Cook all together after being blended for 1 hour on low heat chill and enjoy its hot but irresistible enjoy all.

The flavor of each makes this the best salsa!

Negetive Salsa

Ingredients

- 7 hot pepers
- 3 hot onions
- little chop pepers whit lots an lots of hot salsa

Method for Making Negetive salsa

Put it in the grinder and there you go you got Negiteve salsa!

Well, I do not know what this means but what the heck I tried it! When you take this salsa, your mine is in like a different world you feal like drinking water all day.

Basic Salsa with Any Kind of Dry Chiles

Ingredients

Yield: 4 servings

- 6 lg Chiles dry (morita or mulato
- Or guajillo or any kind) if the chiles are littles like Jalapeños or serranos, use 15 chiles
- 1/2 md Onion
- 1/4 c Vinegar
- 1 sm Clove of garlic
- Salt
- Vegetable oil

Method

The kind of chiles that you use determine the final flavor, you can experiment with different kinds or mixing the different kinds of chiles.

But this is the basic recipe for prepare salsas with dry chiles.

Fresh Tomato Salsa

Ingredients

Yield: 3 cups

- 3 md Tomatoes, seeded, chopped, (about 3 cups)
- 1/2 c Sliced green onions (w/tops)
- 1/2 c Chopped green bell pepper
- 2 tb To 3 tb lime juice
- 2 tb Snipped fresh cilantro
- 1 tb Finely chopped jalapeno
- 1 ts Finely chopped galic (about 3 cloves)
- 1/2 ts Salt

Method

Mix all ingredients.

Watermelon Salsa

Ingredients

- 1 Watermelon
- 1 bn Cilantro
- 1 c Balsamic Vinegar
- 1 Red Onion

Method

Halve the watermelon, scoop out meat. Seed (this took forever!) cut up into presentable pieces, not too big.

Save one of the halves to serve the salsa in. Reserve some of the watermelon juice.

Chop cilantro (watch out for stems!) Chop onion.

Amounts will depend on size of the watermelon.

White Salsa

Ingredients

- 1 c Mayonnaise
- 1 c Sour cream
- 3 Limes, juice only
- 1-1/2 c Chopped cilantro
- 4 Cloves garlic, minced
- 1-1/2 c Chopped scallions
- 1 cn (15 oz) sliced black olives
- 1/2 ts Tabasco

Method

Mix and refrigerate. Let flavors marry for at least 4 hours.

Adobo Herb Salsa

Ingredients

- 1 (28 ounce) can diced tomatoes
- 1 green bell pepper, diced
- 1/4 cup minced red onion
- 1/4 cup minced fresh cilantro
- 1 tablespoon adobo sauce from canned chipotle peppers
- 1 tablespoon chopped fresh tarragon
- 1/2 teaspoon salt
- 2 tablespoons balsamic vinegar

Method

In a bowl, toss together the tomatoes, bell pepper, onion, cilantro, adobo sauce, tarragon, and vinegar.

Season to taste with salt, cover, and refrigerate at least 30 minutes.

Artichoke Salsa

Ingredients

- 1 (6.5 ounce) jar marinated artichoke hearts, drained and chopped
- 3 Roma (plum) tomatoes, chopped
- 2 tablespoons chopped red onion
- 1/4 cup chopped black olives
- 1 tablespoon chopped garlic
- 2 tablespoons chopped fresh basil
- salt and pepper to taste

Method

In a medium bowl, mix artichoke hearts, tomatoes, onion, olives, garlic, salt, and pepper.

Serve chilled, or at room temperature, with tortilla chips.

Beef and Salsa Dip

Ingredients

- 1 pound ground beef
- 1 (16 ounce) jar salsa
- 1 (8 ounce) container sour cream
- 1/2 head iceberg lettuce - rinsed, dried, and shredded
- 1/2-pound shredded Cheddar cheese

Method

Place ground beef in a large skillet. Cook and stir over medium heat until browned. Drain off excess fat.

Stir in salsa, and simmer over low heat for 10 minutes.

Pat cooked meat into bottom of a pie plate, cover, and refrigerate. When meat is completely chilled, spread sour cream over meat.

Arrange lettuce evenly over sour cream, and top with Cheddar cheese.

Black Bean Salsa

Ingredients

- 3 (15 ounce) cans black beans, drained and rinsed
- 1 (11 ounce) can Mexican-style corn, drained
- 2 (10 ounce) cans diced tomatoes with green chile peppers, partially drained
- 2 tomatoes, diced
- 2 bunches green onions, chopped
- cilantro leaves, for garnish

Method

In a large bowl, mix black beans, Mexican-style corn, diced tomatoes with green chile peppers, tomatoes and green onion stalks.

Garnish with desired amount of cilantro leaves.

Chill in the refrigerator at least 8 hours, or overnight, before serving.

Black Beans con Jalapeno

Ingredients

- 1 (15 ounce) can white hominy, drained
- 1 (15 ounce) can black beans, rinsed and drained
- 1 cup diced white onion
- 1 cup diced green bell pepper
- 1 cup diced red bell pepper
- 1 cup diced green onions with tops
- 1/4 cup seeded and chopped jalapeno pepper
- 1 (24 ounce) jar picante sauce
- 2 tablespoons ground cumin
- 1 tablespoon salt
- 2 tablespoons white sugar
- 1/2 cup finely chopped cilantro

Method

In a large bowl, gently stir together the hominy, black beans, onion, green and red peppers, green onion, jalapeno, picante sauce, cumin, salt, sugar and cilantro. Refrigerate at least an hour before serving. Serve with tortilla chips on a bed of lettuce.

Black-Eyed Pea Salsa

Ingredients

- 1 cup white rice
- 2 cups water
- 2 (15.5 ounce) cans black-eyed peas, drained and rinsed
- 1 (10 ounce) can diced tomatoes with green chile peppers

Method

Bring a small pot of rice and water to a boil. Cover pot, reduce heat to simmer and let cook 20 minutes or until rice is tender.

In a large saucepan, combine rice, peas, tomatoes and chili. Stir the mixture over a medium heat until it is heated through.

Citrus Salsa

Ingredients

- 4 Roma tomatoes
- 2 large oranges, peeled and diced
- 1 large Vidalia onion, peeled and chopped
- 2 jalapeno peppers, seeded and minced
- 2 tablespoons fresh lime juice
- 1/4 cup fresh orange juice
- 3 (1 gram) packets SPLENDA®
- 1 tablespoon chopped fresh cilantro
- 1 teaspoon salt

Method

Bring small saucepan of water to a boil. Blanch tomatoes for 30 seconds, and then rinse with cold water. Peel and chop tomatoes.

Place all ingredients in a large bowl and stir until mixed thoroughly. Allow to stand at room temperature for one hour. Mix and serve. Refrigerate any unused salsa.

Corn and Bean Salsa with Avocado

Ingredients

- 1 (16 ounce) package Cascadian Farm® frozen organic sweet corn, thawed and drained
- 1 (14.5 ounce) can Muir Glen® organic diced tomatoes, drained
- 1 (15 ounce) can black beans, rinsed and drained
- 1 avocado, pitted, peeled and chopped
- 1/2 cup chopped red onions
- 1 clove garlic, finely chopped
- 2 tablespoons chopped fresh cilantro
- 2 tablespoons red wine vinegar
- 1 tablespoon vegetable oil
- 1 teaspoon ground cumin
- 1/2 teaspoon salt
- 1/4 teaspoon pepper

Method

Stir together all ingredients. Refrigerate until ready to serve.

CPSIA information can be obtained
at www.ICGtesting.com
Printed in the USA
BVHW051352080321
601998BV00011BA/1359

9 781914 405259